Krzysztof Penderecki

Krzysztof Penderecki

A GUIDE TO HIS WORKS

Ray Robinson

Prestige Publications, Inc.

Princeton, New Jersey 08540

The musical example on the cover is taken from the orchestral work *Polymorphia* (1961). © 1963 by Hermann Moeck Verlag, Celle, West Germany. Used by permission of European American Music Distribution Corporation, sole United States agent for Moeck Verlag.

This introduction to the life and work of Krzysztof Penderecki (b. 1933) has been compiled in recognition of the composer's fiftieth birthday on November 23, 1983. Though books dealing with Penderecki have been published in Polish and German, there is not a single book or scholarly article in the English language that recognizes the special contribution he has made to the music of our time. This volume seeks to begin the process of filling this gap.

Prestige Publications, Inc., will soon release a book by Ray Robinson and Allen Winold on the Penderecki *Passion According to St. Luke* (1965-66).

EDITOR

Table of Contents

I	*A Short Biographical Sketch*	1
II	*Style Periods*	5
III	*List of Works*	8
	Chamber music	8
	Choral	8
	Electronic tape	10
	Jazz Ensemble	11
	Opera	11
	Orchestral	11
	Solo instrument with orchestra	13
	Symphonic wind ensemble	14
IV	*First Performances*	15
V	*Discography*	22
VI	*Chronology*	28
	Notes	32
	Bibliography	33

I
A Short Biographical Sketch

Krzysztof Penderecki stands today at the apex of a career which has attracted the attention of the musical connoisseur and the general public alike in Europe, America, and most recently in South America and Japan. Initially recognized as the leader of a potent and creative avant-garde movement in Poland in the early-1960's, Penderecki has gone on to establish himself as one of the most important composers and conductors in the world today.

Born on November 23, 1933 in the provincial city of Dębica, Penderecki's formative years were spent in a small Polish town during a period of national suffering and political turmoil. As a child he witnessed some of the devastating effects of the German occupation of Poland. The atrocities of Auschwitz took place in his own back yard. The domination and suppression of the Communists began during his teenage years. Since he lived in Poland during this period, he experienced firsthand the horror and terror of the times. These events could not help but influence his compositional output and shape his highly-charged, intensely emotional scores.

Because he was raised in a devout Roman Catholic home, religion rather than music dominated his early life. "Until I was fifteen I was perhaps overly devout," Penderecki told an interviewer for *Newsweek* magazine (March 17, 1969). "I had begun reading Augustine and Aquinas. My mother wanted me to go into the church. In our hometown the church was absolutely the center of life. People would kiss the shoulder of the priest as he walked by."[1] It is clear that Penderecki's interest in the church and in sacred texts was developed during his early years.

Penderecki's musical interests were nurtured in early childhood by a family in which the arts occupied an important place. With the encouragement of his parents, he studied both the piano and violin. There were no professional musicians in the family but a great deal of amateur music making occurred in the home while he was still a young boy. His father, who was a lawyer by profession, and various uncles played duets and quartets during their leisure hours. With the passing years Penderecki's attachment to the violin became more serious while his interest in the piano waned.

Upon the completion of basic schooling in his hometown, Penderecki went to Krakow in 1951 to enter the university and to study art, literature and philosophy. His interests focused on classical antiquity. Parallel to his university studies ran his musical training at the Krakow Conservatory. Here he resumed the violin studies he had begun after the war and made his first informal attempts at composition. By 1953, his musical interests had developed to the extent that he enrolled in compositional studies at the Conservatory with Franciszek Skolyszewski. His personal debt to Skolyszewski was expressed in an interview in 1968 when he stated: "I owe my entire musical development to him, for it was he who discovered my talent and encouraged me."[2]

With the support of his teacher, and with the growing realization that he had something important to say as a composer, Penderecki abandoned his university studies in 1954 to enter the State Academy of Music in Krakow and to pursue serious study for a career as a composer. It was here that he came under the influence of Artur Malawski (1904-1957) and Stanislaw Wiechowicz (1893-1963). Malawski, the principal composition teacher at the Academy, was an adventurous composer who maintained a healthy balance between contemporary techniques and the musical tradition. He was active in the International Society for Contemporary Music (ISCM). As a teacher he required his students to master the craft of composition during their study under his tutelage.

Acknowledging his indebtedness to Malawski some years later, Penderecki echoed his teacher's compositional philosophy: "The general principles at the root of a work's musical style, the logic and economy of development, and the integrity of a musical experience embodied in the notes the composer is setting down on

2

paper, never change. The idea of good music means today exactly what it meant always."[3] It is obvious that tradition was important to Penderecki, even during his student years.

After Malawski's death in 1957, Wiechowicz succeeded him as Penderecki's principal teacher at the Academy. During these student years, Penderecki composed some conservative works for small ensembles, "Two Songs for Baritone and Piano" (1955), a "String Quartet" (1955) and a set of *Three Miniatures for Clarinet* (1956), which later became his earliest published work (Polskie Wydawnictwo Muzyczne, 1958). He earned his diploma *cum laude* from the Academy in 1958, after submitting as his graduation composition a two-movement work entitled "Epitaph on the Death of Malawski" for strings and timpani. This piece received its premiere at a concert of the Krakow Philharmonic Orchestra, Michael Baranowski, conductor.

Penderecki's early professional life consisted primarily of teaching and composing. He was appointed to the faculty of the Academy in the fall of 1958 as a teacher of counterpoint and composition. To earn extra money he also lectured at the Krakow Theological Seminary and served as a correspondent for the magazine, *Ruch Muzyczny*, in which he wrote—not as a critic, but as a journalist—a column entitled "Performances of New Works." While working in this way in 1959, he entered three of his newest compositions in the Second Competition for Young Composers in Warsaw. Suddenly the musical world was aware that here was an unusual talent as his works won all three prizes: *Strophes* (1959) took a first prize while *Emanations* and the *Psalms of David* earned second prizes (both were composed in 1958). The following year his music was revealed to the world outside Poland for the first time as *Anaklasis* (1960), for strings and percussion, was heard in West Germany at the Donaueschingen Festival, the first of five works to be commissioned by that Festival. One year later, *Threnody to the Victims of Hiroshima* (1959-61) was singled out by the *Tribune Internationale des Compositeurs* in Paris as one of the outstanding works of the year.

With the appearance of *Stabat Mater* (1962) and the premiere of the *St. Luke Passion* at the Cathedral of Münster, West Germany,

3

on March 30, 1966, a date which the critic Wolfram Schwinger says now belongs among the significant dates of music history, Penderecki moved to a new phase of maturity and recognition. On the strength of St. Luke alone, Penderecki would be assured a place among the important composers of the twentieth century, but he has not stopped here: he has gone on to score impressive triumphs in chamber music, opera and orchestral works, while continuing to produce highly effective scores in the field of religious choral music.

Penderecki's compositions are now performed regularly the world over and he has acquired the reputation of being one of the most original creators of his generation. In 1975 he was made an honorary member of the Royal Academies in London and Stockholm and was recognized by the Art Academies of West Berlin and the German Democratic Republic (DDR). He is also a member of the Academy of Science in Bordeaux (France), the Academy of Saint Cecilia in Rome (Italy), and the Academy of Bella Artes in Buenos Aires (Argentina). He has received honorary degrees from the Eastman School of Music, St. Olaf College, the University of Louven (Belgium) and Bordeaux University (France).

Penderecki has also influenced composition students as a teacher at the Academy of Music in Essen, West Germany (1966-68), Yale University in New Haven, Connecticut (1972-78) and the Aspen Music Festival (1977). Since 1972 he has served as Rector of the Academy of Music in Krakow, Poland.

II
Style Periods

Penderecki's compositional output consists of forty-seven published works which fall into the following categories: chamber music (7), choral (14), electronic tape (3 unpublished works), jazz ensemble (1), opera (2), orchestral (14), solo instrument with orchestra (7), and symphonic wind ensemble (2). These works, composed between 1956 and 1982, fall rather clearly into three style periods: exploration (1956-62), stability (1962-64), and expression (1974-   ).[4]

Exploration and experimentation: the search for a new musical language

Even a superficial analysis of the works which were composed between 1956 and 1962 will reveal that Penderecki was searching for new sounds. The very fact that Poland was isolated from the rest of Western Europe in the period after the war (1949-1956) gave him the unique opportunity to develop his own style. For example, it was not until 1957 that he heard his first Stravinsky piece (*Rite of Spring*). In 1958, Luigi Nono made a visit to Poland and brought with him the scores of Schoenberg, Webern, Krenek and Boulez. Nono was an active member of the Communist party in Italy at that time; he went to Poland to find similar ideas in that socialist country. There is no question but that some of these first period works were influenced by Nono's visit and the scores he left with Penderecki. For example, the *Miniatures for Clarinet and Piano* (1956) show the influence of Bartók, the *Psalms of David* (1958) the compositional style of Stravinsky, and the *Miniatures for Violin and Piano* (1959) the model of Webern.

Some have called this period in Polish music *Farbmusik* (lit. color-music), in which a distinctively experimental, avant-garde idiom produced new instrumental and vocal timbres. Some of the characteristics of this new style are free serialism (*Psalms of David*), three-

5

line tempo graph (*Anaklasis*), time-space notation (*Dimensions of Time and Silence*), semi-tonal clusters for sound density (*Threnody*), and new timbres from stringed instruments (*String Quartet #1*). The spectra of sound in these works are fascinating: the use of densely-packed groups of quarter and three-quarter tones; the fanning out of broad bands of sound; string glissandi in clusters moving in opposite directions simultaneously; and the producing of string sounds close to the bridge, behind the bridge, under the strings, and on the wood of the instrument. The orchestral work *Fluorescences* (1962) takes this direction to an extreme.

These experiments with a new musical language brought with them the necessity of a whole new system of notation. It was Penderecki who pioneered in the development of the avant-garde notation that became part of the new musical language of the 1960's. These new notational symbols are now used by composers everywhere.

Stability: an emerging personal style

With the premiere of the a cappella choral work *Stabat Mater* (1962), a new style in Penderecki's compositions begins to emerge. He had gone about as far as he could go in the direction of experimenting with sound. The search had reached its climax in *Kanon* (1962), for string orchestra and two tape recorders, and *Fluorescences*. Penderecki himself recognized that he was at an important crossroads. "The solution to my dilemma," he stated in an interview, "was not to go forward and perhaps destroy the whole spirit of music as a result, but to gain inspiration from the past and to look back on my heritage."[5] He now began the search for stability and a personal style.

Here he was taking a new path, but not without some backward glances: new sound-surfaces entered into meaningful relationships with traditional elements of form (*St. Luke Passion*), melodic materials in Gregorian style blended with boldly inventive layers of sound (*Stabat Mater*), and the earlier experiments in controlled rhythm settled into a more indeterminate rhythmic character (*De Natura Sonoris #1*). In this period, serialism as a tonal context is abandoned

6

for modal, diatonic and quarter-tone material, the sometimes fragmented sound events of the earlier years flower into polyphonic idioms, and a generally more evenly balanced style emerges.

While the writing of the first period had explored sound sources which were possible with instruments (primarily strings), the scores which appear between the years 1962 and 1974 reveal similar practices with vocal sonorities. This type of experimentation reaches its culmination with *Canticum Canticorum Salomonis* (1972-73), a work which takes the search for vocal sounds to the same kind of extreme that *Fluorescences* reveals with instrumental writing. Not surprisingly, Penderecki's most important choral works to date come from this period: *Stabat Mater* (1962), *St. Luke Passion* (1965-66), *Dies Irae* (1967), *Utrenia* (1970-71), and *Kosmogonia* (1970).

Expression: works in the style of post-Wagnerian chromaticism

In the summer of 1974, Penderecki completed a short work for chamber orchestra and 12 ocarinas which signaled a new compositional style. Entitled *The Awakening of Jacob*, and inspired by the famous biblical account, this mystical and poetical piece introduces the elements of melody and harmony as serious devices for the first time in the composer's work. Gone is the experimental writing of the early years; missing is the indeterminate avant-garde style of the middle period. In their place is a dramatic and passionate idiom which owes much to post-Wagnerian chromaticism with its expressive melodic lines, its lyrical outpouring, and its dramatic highlights. The *Violin Concerto* (1976), which is firmly rooted in the tradition of Brahms and Sibelius, and the powerful opera *Paradise Lost* (1978) confirm this style. In the words of Wolfram Schwinger, "the composer has moved from the realm of tonal planes to the realm of melody."[6]

III
List of Works

CHAMBER MUSIC

MINIATURES for Clarinet and Piano (1956) 10'20"
    Publisher: Polskie Wydawnictwo Muzyczne (PWM)[7]
    (Polish Music Publishers), Krakow, Poland
MINIATURES for Violin and Piano (1959) 7'
    Publisher: Belwin Mills, New York, New York
STROPHES for Soprano, Speaker and Instrumental Ensemble (1959)
    8'
    Publisher: Belwin Mills
    Written for the Second Competition for Young Composers in
    Warsaw, Poland. This work won the first prize, 1959.
STRING QUARTET #1 (1960) 7'40"
    Publisher: Belwin Mills
STRING QUARTET #2 (1968) 10'
    Publisher: B. Schott Söhne, Mainz, West Germany
CAPRICCIO for Siegfried Palm for Violoncello Solo (1968) 10'
    Publisher: Schott
    Commissioned by Siegfried Palm
CAPRICCIO for Tuba (1980) 8'
    Publisher: Schott

CHORAL MUSIC

PSALMS OF DAVID for Mixed Chorus and Percussion (1958) 10'
    Publisher: Moeck Verlag, Celle, West Germany
DIMENSIONS OF TIME AND SILENCE for Mixed Chorus, Stringed In-
    struments and Percussion (1959-60) 8'40"
    Publisher: Moeck

STABAT MATER for 3 Sixteen Part A Cappella Choruses (1962) 8'30"
Publisher: Belwin Mills
Written for the Celebration of the Polskie Wydawnictwo Mu-
zyczyne Publishing House in Krakow, Poland

CANTATA for 2 Mixed Choruses and Orchestra (In honorem Almae
Matris Universitatis Iagellonicae) (1964) 6'
Publisher: Belwin Mills
Written for the 600th Anniversary of the founding of the Uni-
versity of Krakow, Poland

PASSION ACCORDING TO ST. LUKE for 3 Soloists, Speaker, 3 Mixed
Choruses, Boy Choir and Orchestra (1965-66) 80'
Publisher: Moeck
Commissioned by the Northwest German Radio, Cologne, on
the occasion of the 700th Anniversary of the Münster Cathe-
dral, West Germany

DIES IRAE for 3 Soloists (Soprano, Tenor, Bass), Mixed Chorus and
Orchestra (1967) 22'
Publisher: Moeck
Written for the unveiling of the International Monument to
the Victims of Fascism at Auschwitz-Birkenau, Poland

UTRENIA, Part I, "Grablegung Christi" ("The Burial of Christ") for
5 Soloists, 2 Mixed Choruses and Orchestra (1969-70) 50'
Publisher: Schott
Commissioned by the Northwest German Radio, Cologne,
West Germany

UTRENIA, Part II, "Auferstehung Christi" ("The Resurrection of
Christi") for 5 Soloists, 2 Mixed Choruses, Boy Choir and Or-
chestra (1970-71) 36'
Publisher: Schott
Commissioned by the Northwest German Radio, Cologne,
West Germany

KOSMOGONIA for 4 Soloists, Mixed Chorus and Orchestra (1970) 20'
Publisher: Schott
Commissioned by the United Nations on the occasion of the
25th Anniversary of its founding, New York, New York

ECLOGA VIII for 6 Male Voices (1972) 8'
   Publisher: Schott
   Commissioned by the Edinburgh Festival, Edinburgh, Scotland

CANTICUM CANTICORUM SALOMONIS for 16 Voice Mixed Chorus, Chamber Orchestra and 2 Dancers (optional) (1972-73) 17'
   Publisher: Schott
   Commissioned by the Gulbenkian Foundation, Lisbon, Portugal

MAGNIFICAT for Bass Solo, 7 Male Voices, 2 Mixed Choruses, Boy Choir and Orchestra (1974) 37'
   Publisher: Schott
   Commissioned by the Salzburg Festival, Austria

PRELUDE, VISIONS AND FINALE from *Paradise Lost* for 6 Soloists, Large Mixed Chorus and Orchestra (1979) 40'
   Publisher: Schott

TE DEUM for 4 Soloists (Soprano, Alto, Tenor, Bass), Mixed Chorus and Orchestra (1980) 35'
   Publisher: Schott
   Written for Pope John Paul II

LACRYMOSA for Soprano Solo, Mixed Chorus and Orchestra (1981) 7'
   Publisher: Schott
   Commissioned by Lech Walesa and the Solidarity Labor Movement for the Memorial Service Unveiling the Monument honoring the 28 Polish workers who were killed in the riots of 1970, Gdansk, Poland.

AGNUS DEI for Mixed Chorus A Cappella (1981) 10'
   Publisher: Schott
   Written for the Funeral of Stefán Cardinal Wyszynski, Warsaw, Poland

ELECTRONIC TAPE

PSALM 1961 for 2 Tape Recorders (1961) 5'05"
   Unpublished

Written for the Fylkingen Concert Series in Stockholm, Sweden

TODESBRIGADE for Electronic Tape (1963)
Unpublished
Written for the Polish Radio, Warsaw, Poland

EKECHIRIA for Electronic Tape (1972)
Unpublished
Written for the Opening Ceremony of the 1972 Olympic Games, Munich, West Germany

JAZZ ENSEMBLE

ACTIONS for Jazz Ensemble (1971) 17'
Publisher: Schott
Commissioned by the Donaueschingen Festival, West Germany

OPERA

THE DEVILS OF LOUDUN (1968-69) 120'
Publisher: Schott
Commissioned by the Hamburg State Opera, West Germany

PARADISE LOST (1978) 180'
Publisher: Schott
Commissioned by the Chicago Lyric Opera Company, Chicago, Illinois

ORCHESTRAL

EPITAPH ON THE DEATH OF ARTUR MALAWSKI for Orchestra (1958)
Unpublished
Written as the Diploma Piece for the State Academy of Music, Krakow, Poland

EMANATIONS for 2 String Orchestras (1958) 8'
Publisher: Moeck

ANAKLASIS for 42 Strings and Percussion (1960) 9'
Publisher: Moeck
Written for the Donaueschingen Festival, West Germany

11

THRENODY for 52 Strings (1960) 8'26"
    Publisher: Belwin Mills
    Written as a contest piece under the title 8'26", and later dedicated "For the Victims of Hiroshima"
POLYMORPHIA for 48 Strings (1961) 10'45"
    Publisher: Moeck
    Commissioned by the North German Radio, Hamburg, West Germany
KANON for String Orchestra and 2 Tape Recorders (1962) 8'20"
    Publisher: Schott
FLUORESCENCES for Orchestra (1962) 13'15"
    Publisher: Moeck
    Commissioned by the Southwest German Radio, Baden-Baden, West Germany
DE NATURA SONORIS #1 for Orchestra (1966) 7'40"
    Publisher: Moeck
    Commissioned by the International Festival, Rouen, France
DE NATURA SONORIS #2 for Orchestra (1971) 10'
    Publisher: Schott
    Commissioned by the Juilliard School of Music, New York, New York
PARTITA for Harpsichord, 4 Amplified Instruments and Orchestra (1972) 19'
    Publisher: Schott
    Commissioned by the Eastman School of Music, Rochester, New York
SYMPHONY #1 (1973) 30'
    Publisher: Schott
    Commissioned by the Perkins Engine Company, Peterborough, England
INTERMEZZO for 24 Strings (1973) 6'
    Publisher: Schott
    Commissioned by the Zurich Chamber Orchestra, Switzerland
THE AWAKENING OF JACOB for Orchestra (1974) 8'
    Publisher: Schott

12

Commissioned by Prince Rainier III on the occasion of the 25th Anniversary of his ascendancy to the throne of Monaco, Monte Carlo, Monaco

ADAGIETTO from *Paradise Lost* for Orchestra (1979) 5'
Publisher: Schott

SYMPHONY #2 ("Christmas Symphony") (1979-80) 35'
Publisher: Schott
Commissioned by the New York Philharmonic, New York

SOLO INSTRUMENTS WITH ORCHESTRA

FONOGRAMMI for Flute and Chamber Orchestra (1961) 6'30"
Publisher: Moeck
Written for the Bianale Festival in Venice, Italy

SONATA FOR VIOLONCELLO and Orchestra (1964) 10'
Publisher: Belwin Mills
Commissioned by the Donaueschingen Festival, West Germany

CAPRICCIO FOR OBOE and 11 Strings (1965) 6'45"
Publisher: Moeck
Commissioned by the Lucerne Festival, Switzerland

CAPRICCIO FOR VIOLIN and Orchestra (1967) 10'
Publisher: Moeck
Commissioned by the Donaueschingen Festival, West Germany

CONCERTO #1 FOR VIOLONCELLO and Orchestra (1972) 20'
Publisher: Moeck
Rewritten version of the Concerto for Violino Grande
The Violoncello Concerto was composed for the Edinburgh Festival, Edinburgh, Scotland

CONCERTO FOR VIOLIN and Orchestra (1976) 40'
Publisher: Schott
Commissioned by the Allgemeine Musikgesellschaft, Basel, Switzerland

CONCERTO #2 FOR VIOLONCELLO and Orchestra (1982)
Publisher: Schott
Commissioned by the Berlin Philharmonic Orchestra, Berlin,
West Germany

SYMPHONIC WIND ENSEMBLE

PITTSBURGH OVERTURE for Wind Instruments (1967) 12'
Publisher: C. F. Peters, New York, New York
Commissioned by the American Wind Symphony, Pittsburgh,
Pennsylvania
PRELUDE for Winds, Percussion and Contrabasses (1971) 8'
Publisher: Schott
Commissioned by the Dutch Radio, Amsterdam, Holland

IV
First Performances

EPITAPH ON THE DEATH OF A. MALAWSKI for Orchestra (1958)
Krakow Philharmonic Orchestra, Michael Baranowski, conductor, Philharmonic Hall, Krakow, Poland, June 1958 (Unpublished diploma piece for the State Academy of Music)

3 MINIATURES for Clarinet and Piano (1956)
Władyslaw Kosieradski, clarinet, Zbigniew Jezewski, piano. Union of Composers Concert, Krakow, Poland, November 17, 1958

PSALMS OF DAVID for Mixed Chorus and Percussion (1958)
Krakow Philharmonic Chorus and Orchestra, Andrzej Markowski, conductor, Philharmonic Hall, Krakow, Poland, October 9, 1959

EMANATIONS for Two String Orchestras (1958)
West German Radio Orchestra of Frankfurt, Michael Gielen, conductor, Darmstadt Summer Festival, Darmstadt, West Germany, September 7, 1961

STROPHES for Soprano, Speaker and 10 Instruments (1959)
Chamber Orchestra of the Schlesieschen Philharmonic, Andrzej Markowski, conductor, Zofia Stachurska, soprano, Franciszek Delekta, speaker, Warsaw Autumn Festival, Warsaw, Poland, September 17, 1959

MINIATURES for Violin and Piano (1959)
Henryk Jarzyński, violin, Krzysztof Penderecki, piano, State Academy of Music Concert Hall, Krakow, Poland (Concert organized by the Polish Publishing House, Polskie Wydawnictwo Muzyczne), June, 1960

ANAKLASIS for 42 Strings and Percussion (1959-60)
Southwest German Radio Orchestra, Hans Rosbaud, conductor, Donaueschingen Festival, Donaueschingen, West Germany, October 22, 1960

15

DIMENSIONS OF TIME AND SILENCE for Mixed Chorus, String Instruments, and Percussion (1959-60)
First setting: Krakow Philharmonic Chorus and Orchestra, Andrzej Markowski, conductor, Krakow, Poland, September 18, 1960; Second setting: RIAS-Chamber Chorus and Instrumental Ensemble, Friedrich Cerha, conductor, Vienna, Austria, June, 1961

THRENODY for 52 Strings (1960)
Krakow Philharmonic Symphony Orchestra, Witold Rowicki, conductor, Warsaw, Poland, May 31, 1961

STRING QUARTET #1 (1960)
LaSalle String Quartet, Cincinnati, Ohio (USA), May 11, 1962

PSALM 1961 for 2 Tape Recorders (1961)
Work for electronic tape, Stockholm, Sweden, April 10, 1961 (Unpublished)

FONOGRAMMI for Flute and Chamber Orchestra (1961)
Stanislaw Marony, flute, Krakow Chamber Orchestra, Andrzej Markowski, conductor, Bianale Festival, Venice, Italy, September 24, 1961

POLYMORPHIA for 48 Strings (1961)
North German Radio Orchestra, Hamburg, West Germany, Andrzej Markowski, conductor, April 16, 1962

KANON for String Orchestra and 2 Tape Recorders (1962)
Polish Radio Symphony Orchestra, Jan Krenz, conductor, Warsaw, Poland, September 21, 1962

FLUORESCENCES for Orchestra (1962)
Southwest German Radio Orchestra, Hans Rosbaud, conductor, Donaueschingen Festival, Donaueschingen, West Germany, October 21, 1962

STABAT MATER for 3 Sixteen Part A Cappella Choruses (1962)
Warsaw Philharmonic Chorus, Antoni Szaliński, conductor. Concert organized by the Polish Publishing House, PWM, Krakow, Poland, November 27, 1962

16

TODESBRIGADE for Electronic Tape (1963)
Concert performance in Warsaw, Poland, January 20, 1964
(Unpublished)

CANTATA for 2 Mixed Choruses and Orchestra (In honorem Almae
Matris Universitatis Iagellonicae) (1964)
Warsaw Philharmonic Chorus and Orchestra, Witold Rowicki,
conductor, Warsaw, Poland, May 10, 1964

SONATA for Violoncello and Orchestra (1964)
Southwest German Radio Orchestra, Siegfried Palm, violoncello, Ernest Bour, conductor, Donaueschingen Festival, Donaueschingen, West Germany, October 18, 1964

CAPRICCIO for Oboe and 11 Strings (1965)
Lucerne Orchestra, Heinz Holliger, oboe, Rudolf Baumgart-
ner, conductor, Lucerne Festival, Switzerland, August 26, 1965

PASSION ACCORDING TO ST. LUKE (1965-66)
Cologne Radio Chorus and Orchestra, Tölzer Boys Choir,
Henryk Czyż, conductor, Münster Cathedral, Münster, West
Germany, March 30, 1966. Stefania Woytowicz, Andrzej Hiol-
ski, Bernard Ładysz, Rudolf Jürgen Bartsch, Kölner Rund-
funkchor (Herbert Schernue), Tölzer Knabenchor (Gerhard
Schmidt)

DE NATURA SONORIS #1 for Orchestra (1966)
International Festival of Contemporary Art, Rouen, ORTF Orchestra of Paris, France, Andrzej Markowski, conductor, April
7, 1966

DIES IRAE for Solo, Chorus and Orchestra (1967)
Krakow Philharmonic Chorus and Orchestra, Delfina Ambroziak, soprano, Wiesław Ochman, tenor, Bernard Ładysz, bass,
Krzysztof Missona, conductor. Performed at the unveiling of
the International Monument to the Victims of Fascism at
Auschwitz-Birkenau, Poland, April 6, 1967. (The performance
in Krakow on April 14, 1967)

CONCERTO FOR VIOLINO GRANDE AND ORCHESTRA (1966-67)
Bronisław Eichenholtz, Violino grande, Stockholm Philhar-

monic Orchestra, Henryk Czyż, conductor, Östersund, Sweden, July 1, 1967 (Unpublished work written as the Concerto for Violoncello and Orchestra)

PITTSBURGH OVERTURE for Symphonic Wind Ensemble (1967)
American Wind Symphony Orchestra, Robert Austin Boudreau, conductor, Oakmount Riverside Park, Pittsburgh, Pennsylvania, June 30, 1967

CAPRICCIO FOR VIOLIN AND ORCHESTRA (1967)
Wanda Wiłkomirska, violin, Southwest German Radio Orchestra, Ernest Bour, conductor, Donaueschingen Festival, Donaueschingen, West Germany, October 22, 1967

CAPRICCIO FOR SIEGFRIED PALM for Violoncello Solo (1968)
Siegfried Palm, violoncello, Pro Nova Musica 68, Bremen, West Germany, May 4, 1968

DEVILS OF LOUDON (1968-69)
Hamburg State Opera, Hamburg, West Germany, Henryk Czyż, conductor, June 20, 1969

UTRENIA Part I, "The Death of Christ" (1969-70) for 5 Soloists, 2 Mixed Choruses and Orchestra. Stefania Woytowicz, Krystyna Szczepańska, Louis Devos, Bernard Ładysz, Boris Carmeli. Hamburg Radio Choir (Helmut Franz), Chorus and Orchestra of the West German Radio, Altenburg Cathedral, Andrzej Markowski, conductor, Altenburg, West Germany, April 8, 1970

UTRENIA Part II, "The Resurrection of Christ," for 5 Soloists, 2 Mixed Choruses, and Orchestra (1970-71). Chorus and Orchestra of the West German Radio, Tölzer Knabenchor. Münster Cathedral, Andrzej Markowski, conductor, Münster, West Germany, May 28, 1971

STRING QUARTET #2 (1968)
Parrenin Quartet, Berlin, West Germany, September 30, 1970

KOSMOGONIA for Soli, Chorus, and Orchestra (1970)
Johanna Neal, soprano, Robert Nagy, tenor, Bernard Ładysz, bass. Los Angeles Philharmonic Orchestra, Rutgers University

18

Choir (F. Austin Walter), Zubin Mehta, conductor. Performed on the 25th anniversary of the United Nations, New York, New York, October 24, 1970

DE NATURA SONORIS #2 for Orchestra (1971)
The Juilliard Orchestra, Jorge Mester, conductor, New York, New York, December 3, 1972

PRELUDE FOR WINDS, PERCUSSION, AND CONTRABASSES (1971)
Dutch Radio Wind Ensemble, Hans Vonk, conductor, Concertgebouw, Amsterdam, Holland, July 4, 1971

ACTIONS for Jazz Ensemble (1971)
Globe Unity Orchestra, Krzysztof Penderecki, conductor, Donaueschingen Festival, Donaueschingen, West Germany, October 17, 1971

PARTITA for Harpsichord, Electric Guitar, Bass Guitar, Double Bass, and Chamber Orchestra (1971-72)
Eastman Rochester Philharmonic, Walter Hendl, conductor, Felicia Blumenthal, harpsichord, Rochester, New York, February 11, 1972

ECLOGA VIII for 6 Male Voices (1972)
The King's Singers, Edinburgh Festival, Edinburgh, Scotland, August 21, 1972

EKECHIRIA for Electronic Tape (1972)
Opening Ceremony for the Olympic Games, Munich, West Germany, August 26, 1972 (Unpublished)

CONCERTO #1 FOR VIOLONCELLO AND ORCHESTRA (1972)
Siegfried Palm, violoncello, Scottish National Orchestra, Alexander Gibson, conductor, Edinburgh Festival, Scotland, September 21, 1972

CANTICUM CANTICORUM SALOMONIS for 16 Voice Mixed Chorus, Chamber Orchestra, and 2 Dancers (optional) (1972-73)
NCRV Vocal Ensemble, Percussion Ensemble of Strasbourg, Orchestra of the Gulbenkian Foundation, Werner Andreas Albert, conductor, Lisbon, Portugal, June 5, 1973

SYMPHONY #1 (1973)
London Symphony Orchestra, Krzysztof Penderecki, conductor, Peterborough Cathedral, Peterborough, England, July 19, 1973

INTERMEZZO for 24 Strings (1973)
Zurich Chamber Orchestra, Edmund de Stoutz, conductor, Zurich, Switzerland, November 30, 1973

THE AWAKENING OF JACOB for Orchestra (1974)
Monte Carlo Orchestra, Stanisław Skrowaczewski, conductor, Monte Carlo, August 14, 1974

MAGNIFICAT for Soli, Two 24-part Mixed Choruses, Boys Chorus, and Orchestra (1973-74)
Peter Lagger, bass, Vienna Boys Choir, Soloists from the Schola Cantorum of Stuttgart, Austrian Radio Chorus and Symphony Orchestra, Krzysztof Penderecki, conductor, Salzburg Festival, Salzburg Cathedral, Austria, August 17, 1974

CONCERTO FOR VIOLIN AND ORCHESTRA (1976-77)
Isaac Stern, violin, Basel Symphony Orchestra, Moshe Atzmon, Basel, Switzerland, April 27, 1977

PARADISE LOST (1975-78) Sacra Rappresentazione in Two Acts
Chicago Lyric Opera, Bruno Bartoletti, conductor; Igal Perrm, Stage Director; Ezio Frigerio, Set Designer; Robert Page, Chorus Master; John Butler, Choreographer. Ellen Shade, William Stone, Peter van Ginkel, Paul Esswood, Joy Davidson. Dancers: Nancy Thuesev, Dennis Wayne, Chicago, Illinois, November 29, 1978

ADAGIETTO from "Paradise Lost" for Orchestra (1979)
Osaka, Japan, May, 1979

SYMPHONY #2 (Christmas Symphony) (1979-80)
New York Philharmonic Symphony Orchestra, Zubin Mehta, conductor, New York, New York, May 1, 1980

CAPRICCIO for Tuba (1980)
Zdzisław Piernik, tuba, Krakow, Poland, June, 1980

20

TE DEUM for 4 Soloists, Mixed Chorus, and Orchestra (1980)
Polish Radio Symphony Orchestra and Chorus, Krzysztof Penderecki, conductor, Assisi, Italy, September 27, 1980. Stefania Woytowicz, Ewa Podles, Paulos Raptis, Bernard Ładysz

LACRYMOSA for Soprano Solo, Mixed Chorus and Orchestra (1981)
Polish Radio Orchestra and Chorus, Antoni Wit, conductor, Gdansk, Poland, December 16, 1981 (This work was pre-recorded and played over loudspeakers at the Gdansk Memorial Service.)

AGNUS DEI for Mixed Chorus A Cappella
Performed on the day of the funeral of Cardinal Stefán Wyszynski, Warsaw Cathedral, Polish Radio Chorus, Antoni Wit, conductor, May 28, 1981. The first concert performance was given by the Choir of the South German Radio, Nürnberg, West Germany, Krzysztof Penderecki, conductor, June 21, 1982

CONCERTO FOR VIOLONCELLO AND ORCHESTRA (1982)
Mishisław Rostroprovich, violoncello, Berlin Philharmonic Symphony Orchestra, Berlin, West Germany, Krzysztof Penderecki, conductor, January 11, 1983

V
Discography

ACTIONS for Jazz Ensemble
The New Eternal Rhythm Orchestra, Krzysztof Penderecki, conductor; Philips 6305 153 D

ANAKLASIS for 42 Strings and Percussion
Warsaw Philharmonic Orchestra, Andrzej Markowski, conductor; Polish Gramophone SXL 0260, Wergo 60020
London Symphony Orchestra, Krzysztof Penderecki, conductor; EMI Electrola SHZE 393

CANTATA for 2 Mixed Choruses and Orchestra
(In honorem Almae Matris Universitatis Iagellonicae)
Philharmonic Orchestra and Chorus of Krakow, Jerzy Katlewicz, conductor; Polish Nagrania SXL 1151

CANTICUM CANTICORUM SALOMONIS for 16 Voice Mixed Chorus, Chamber Orchestra, and 2 Dancers (optional)
Philharmonic Orchestra and Chorus of Krakow, Jerzy Katlewicz, conductor; Polish Nagrania SXL 1151
Polish Radio Symphony Orchestra and Chorus, Krzysztof Penderecki, conductor; EMI Electrola C 065-02484

CAPRICCIO for Oboe and 11 Strings
Heinz Holliger, oboe, Symphony Orchestra of Southwest German Radio, Baden-Baden; Ernest Bour, conductor; Wergo 314

CAPRICCIO for Violin and Orchestra
Wanda Wiłkomirska, violin, National Symphony Orchestra of Poland, Andrzej Markowski, conductor; Polish Gramophone M-3 XW 1033
Paul Zukofsky, violin, Buffalo Philharmonic Orchestra, Lukas Foss, conductor; Nonesuch 71201
Wanda Wiłkomirska, violin, Polish Radio Symphony Orches-

tra, Krzysztof Penderecki, conductor; EMI Electrola C 193-02386/7 Angel S-36950

CONCERTO for Violin and Orchestra

Isaac Stern, violin, Minneapolis Symphony Orchestra, Stanislaw Skrowaczewski, conductor; CBS 76-739

Andrzej Kulka, violin, Polish Radio National Symphony Orchestra, Krzysztof Penderecki, conductor; Polish Gramophone SX 1840

CONCERTO for Violoncello and Orchestra

Siegfried Palm, violoncello, Polish Radio Symphony Orchestra, Krzysztof Penderecki, conductor; EMI Electrola C 193-02386/7 Wergo 60036

DE NATURA SONORIS #1 for Orchestra

Krakow Philharmonic Symphony Orchestra, Henryk Czyż, conductor; Philips 839701 LY

Buffalo Philharmonic Orchestra, Lukas Foss, conductor; Nonesuch, 71201

DE NATURA SONORIS #2 for Orchestra

National Polish Philharmonic Orchestra, Andrzej Markowski, conductor; DISCO M 0781, Philips 6500/683

Louisville Orchestra, Jorge Mester, conductor; Louisville S-722 Polish Radio Symphony Orchestra, Krzysztof Penderecki, conductor; EMI Electrola C 193-02386/7

DEVILS OF LOUDON, Opera in Three Acts

Tatiana Troyanos - *Joanna*; Cvetka Ahlin - *Claire*; Ursula Boese - *Louis*; Andrzej Hiolski - *Grandier*; Bernard Ładysz - *Barré*; Hans Sotin - Rangier; Kurt Marschner - Adam; Heinz Blankenburg - *Mannoury*; Helmut Melchert - *Laubardemont*; Arnold van Mill - Asmodeusz i inni; Choir and Orchestra of the Hamburg State Opera, Marek Janowski, conductor; Philips 6500 050151

DIES IRAE for Soli, Chorus and Orchestra

Stefania Woytowicz, soprano; Wieslaw Ochman, tenor; Bernard Ładysz, bass; Krakow Philharmonic Symphony Orchestra and Chorus, Henryk Czyż, conductor; Philips 839/701 LY

DIMENSIONS OF TIME AND SILENCE for Mixed Chorus, Chamber Orchestra and Percussion
National Philharmonic Orchestra and Chorus, Andrzej Markowski, conductor; DISCO M 0781

ECLOGA VIII
Schola Cantorum Stuttgart, Clytus Gottwald, conductor; Wergo 60070

EMANATIONS for 2 String Orchestras
Polish Radio and Television Symphony Orchestra, Krzysztof Penderecki, conductor; EMI Electrola C 193-02386/7 Angel S-36950
Orchestra of Radio Luxembourg, Alois Springer, conductor; Candide Fox (Fond) CE 31071

FLUORESCENSES for Orchestra
National Polish Philharmonic Orchestra, Warsaw, Andrzej Markowski, conductor; Muza SXL 0260, Wergo 60020, Philips 6500/683

FONOGRAMMI for Flute and Chamber Orchestra
Polish Radio and Television Orchestra, Krzysztof Penderecki, conductor; EI Electrola C 193-02386/7

KANON for String Orchestra and 2 Tape Recorders
Orchestra of the Polish Radio and Television, Krzysztof Penderecki, conductor; EMI Electrola C 193-02386/7

KOSMOGONIA for Soli, Chorus and Orchestra
Stefania Woytowicz, soprano; Kazimierz Pustelak, tenor; Bernard Ładysz, bass; Choir and Orchestra of the National Polish Philharmonic, Warsaw, Andrzej Markowski, conductor; Philips 6500/683

LACRYMOSA
Polish Radio Symphony Orchestra and Chorus of Krakow, Krzysztof Penderecki, conductor; Polish Gramophone SXL

MAGNIFICAT for Soli, 2 Mixed Choruses, Boys Chorus and Orchestra
Polish Radio Orchestra and Chorus of Krakow, Peter Lagger,

bass, Krzysztof Penderecki, conductor; EMI Electrola C 065-02483

MINIATURES for Violin and Piano
Gabriel Banat, violin, Richard Lewis, piano; Turnabout 34429
Gabriel Banat, violin, Ilana Vered, piano; Candide Fox (Fond) CE 31071

MISERERE from the St. Luke Passion
NCRV Vocal Ensemble, Hilversum; M. Voorberg, conductor; Schwan Studio 601
Schola Cantorum of Stuttgart, Clytus Gottwald, conductor; Candide Fox (Fond) CE 31071

PARTITA for Harpsichord, 2 Electronic Guitars, Double Bass and Chamber Orchestra
Felicia Blumental, harpsichord, Polish Radio and Television Symphony Orchestra, Krzysztof Penderecki, conductor; Electrola C 193-02386/7 Angel S-36950

PASSION ACCORDING TO ST. LUKE for Soli, Narrator, Boys Chorus, Mixed Choruses and Orchestra
Stefania Woytowicz, soprano; Andrzej Hiolski, baritone; Bernard Ładysz, bass; Leszek Herdegen, narrator. Krakow Philharmonic Symphony Orchestra and Chorus, Henryk Czyż, conductor; Polish Gramophone SXL 0325/6, Philips 802 771/72 AY
Stefania Woytowicz, soprano; Andrzej Hiolski, baritone; Bernard Ładysz, bass; Rudolf Jürgen Bartsch, narrator. Tölzer Boys Choir, Cologne Radio Orchestra and Chorus, Henryk Czyż, conductor; RCA VICS-6015; BASF JA 293 793 (Harmonia Mund.)

PITTSBURGH OVERTURE for Wind Instruments
Eastman Wind Ensemble, Donald Hunsberger, conductor; DC 2530/063 American Wind Symphony, Robert Austin Boudreau, conductor; Point 101

POLYMORPHIA for 48 Strings
Krakow Philharmonic Symphony Orchestra, Andrzej Markowski, conductor; Polish Gramophone W-876

Krakow Philharmonic Symphony Orchestra, Henryk Czyż, conductor; Philips 839/701 LY

PSALM 1961 for 2 Tape Recorders
Polish Radio Experimental Studio; Philips 6740/001

PSALMS OF DAVID for Mixed Chorus and Percussion
National Philharmonic Chorus, Andrzej Markowski, conductor; Polish Gramophone SXL 0260, Wergo 60020, Supraphon 10951, Mace S-9090
Vocal Ensemble of Kassel, Klaus-Martin Ziegler, conductor; Cantate 658/225

SONATA for Violoncello and Orchestra
Siegfried Palm, violoncello, Philharmonic Symphony Orchestra of Poznan, Andrzej Markowski, conductor; Wergo 60036
Thomas Blees, violoncello, Orchestra of Radio Luxembourg, Alois Springer, conductor; Candide Fox (Fond) CE 31071

STABAT MATER for 3 Sixteen Part Choruses
Krakow Philharmonic Choir, Andrzej Markowski, conductor; Polish Gramophone W-967
Warsaw Philharmonic Choir, Alndrzej Markowski, conductor; Wergo 60020
Concordia Choir, Paul Christiansen, conductor; Mark 2144
Stockholm Radio Choir, Eric Ericson, conductor; Electrola C 063-29075
Soloists from the French Radio Chorus, Marcel Couraud, conductor; Erato STU 70457

STRING QUARTET #1
LaSalle String Quartet; Polish Gramophone SXL 0282
LaSalle String Quartet; DG 104 988
Kohon Quartet; Candide 31071

STROPHES for Soprano, Speaker and Instrumental Ensemble
Stefania Woytowicz, soprano; Andrzej Szalawski, speaker; Krakow Philharmonic Symphony Orchestra, Jerzy Katlewicz, conductor; Polish Gramophone SXL 1151

SYMPHONY #1
London Symphony Orchestra, Krzysztof Penderecki, conductor; EMI Electrola SHZE 393

SYMPHONY #2

Polish Radio Symphony Orchestra, Jacek Kasprzyk, conductor; Polish Gramophone SXL

TE DEUM

Jadwiga Gadulanka, soprano; Ewa Podles, alto; Wiesław Ochman, tenor, Andrzej Hiolski, bass; Polish Radio Symphony Orchestra and Chorus, Krzysztof Penderecki, conductor, Polish Gramophone SXL

THE AWAKENING OF JACOB

Polish Radio Symphony Orchestra, Krzysztof Penderecki, conductor; EMI Electrola C 065-02484

THRENODY for 52 Strings

Polish National Symphony Orchestra, Witold Rowicki, conductor; Polish Gramophone SXL 0171, Philips 839260 DSY, Philips A 02383 L

Polish Radio Symphony Orchestra, Krzysztof Penderecki, conductor; EMI Electrola SHZE 393

Symphony Orchestra of Rome, Bruno Maderna, conductor; RCA VICS-1239, RCA 940044

Electronic Version, Polish Experimental Studio Radio Warsaw; Philips 6740 001

UTRENIA for Soli, 2 Choruses, Boys Chorus and Orchestra

Stefania Woytowicz, soprano; Kerstin Meyer, mezzosoprano; Seth McCoy, tenor; Bernard Ładyz, bass; Peter Lagger, bass; Temple University Choir; (Robert Page), Philadelphia Orchestra, Eugene Ormandy, conductor, RCA LSC 3180

Delfina Ambroziak, soprano; Krystyna Szczepańska, alto; Boris Carmeli, bass; Chorus and Orchestra of the National Philharmonic, Andrzej Markowski, conductor; Polish Gramophone SXL 0889, Philips 670-0065

Stefania Woytowicz, soprano; Krystyna Szczepańska, alto; Kazimierz Pustelak, tenor; Bernard Ładysz, bass; Peter Lagger, bass; Choir of the Boy Scouts with the Choir and Orchestra of the National Polish Philharmonic, Andrzej Markowski, conductor; Polish Gramophone SXL 0890

VI
Chronology

1933 Born in Dębica, Poland, November 23.

1945 Began studying the piano, but continued only a short time.

1947 Showed first serious interest in music; studied violin privately.

1951 Went to Krakow to begin higher education; studied theory and violin privately, and Latin, Greek and Philosophy at the University. Franciszek Skolyszewski was his first theory teacher.

1952 While continuing studies at the University he entered the Conservatory of Music and studied with Skolyszewski.

1954 Enrolled in the Academy of Music, where he studied composition with Artur Malawski. Composed a String Quartet (unpublished). Married his first wife, Barbara.

1955 Composed Two Songs to texts by Leopold Staff for Baritone and Piano (unpublished). A daughter, Diata, was born in Krakow.

1956 Composed *Miniatures* for Clarinet and Piano, the earliest published work.

1957 After the death of Malawski he studied with Stanislaw Wiechowicz. Heard the Stravinsky *Rite of Spring* for the first time.

1958 Composed "Epitaph in Memory of Malawski" (unpublished) as a diploma piece at the Academy. Met Luigi Nono and received an appointment to the faculty of the Academy. *Psalms of David*.

1959 Won first prize in Polish Composers Competition for *Strophes*, second prize for *Emanations* and *Psalms of David*. Prize money supported a six-week trip to Italy, his first to Western Europe. Composed *Miniatures* for Violin and Piano. Began work in the Warsaw Electronic Studio.

1960   *Anaklasis* composed for the Donaueschingen Festival. Lived in Celle with the publisher Hermann Moeck from October to December. *Strophes* performed in Paris. *Dimensions of Time and Silence, Threnody, String Quartet #1.*

1961   Visited Darmstadt for four days. *Psalm 1961, Fonogrammi, Polymorphia.*

1962   *Threnody* received the Polish State Artistic Prize. *Flourescences, Kanon, Stabat Mater.*

1963   Composed incidental music for *King Ubu* (Jarry), Stockholm Marionette Theatre (Not to be confused with the unfinished opera by the same title.)

1964   Named Dozent at the Academy. Wrote incidental music for *Brigade of Death* for a radio drama. *Cantata, Sonata for Cello and Orchestra.*

1965   Married Elizabeth Solecka, June 18. *Capriccio for Oboe and 11 Strings.*

1966   Completed the *Passion According to St. Luke.* Received the Grand Prize from the West German State of Rhineland, Westphalia and the Polish Peace Prize. A son, Lukas, was born in Krakow. Appointed to the faculty of the Hochschule für Musik, Essen (1966-68). Made his first trip to London. *De Natura Sonoris #1.*

1967   Won Prix Italia for the *St. Luke Passion. Dies Irae, Pittsburgh Overture, Concerto for Violino Grande* (unpublished), *Capriccio for Violin and Orchestra.*

1968   Received a fellowship from the Deutsches Akademie (Berlin) (1968-70). *Capriccio for Siegfried Palm for Violoncello Solo, Quartet #2.*

1969   Completed the first opera, *Devils of Loudon.*

1970   Spent the year in Vienna (1970-71). Completed *Utrenia* (Part I), *Kosmogonia.*

1971   New home in Krakow completed in December. *Utrenia* (Part

II), *De Natura Sonoris #2, Prelude for Winds, Percussion and Contrabasses, Actions for Jazz Ensemble.* A daughter, Dominika, was born in Krakow.

1972   Named Professor at the Academy; appointed Rector of the Academy. Taught at Yale University (November 1 - December 15). *Partita for Harpsichord, 4 Amplified Instruments and Orchestra, Ecloga VIII, Ekechiria for Electronic Tape* (unpublished) performed for the Opening Ceremony of the Munich Olympic Games. *Concerto for Violoncello and Orchestra.*

1973   Returned to Yale University in the Spring (April 1 - May 15); began opera "King Ubu" (as yet unfinished); received Doctor of Music, *honoris causa*, from Eastman School of Music. *Canticum Canticorum Salomonis, Symphony #1, Intermezzo for 24 Strings.*

1974   *The Awakening of Jacob, Magnificat.*

1975   Given honorary membership in the Royal Academies of Music, London and Stockholm. Made honorary member of the Arts Academies of West Berlin and the German Democratic Republic. Appointed to a second term as Rector of the Academy of Music in Krakow. Returned to Yale (1975-76).

1976   Conducted works in Japan for the first time. Worked on the Violin Concerto and opera "Paradise Lost."

1977   Conducted a program of works at Carnegie Hall, New York. Returned to Yale (1977-78). *Concerto for Violin and Orchestra.* Gave courses at the Aspen Festival in the summer. Received the J. G. von Herder International Award.

1978·   Completed opera for the Chicago Lyric Opera, *Paradise Lost: La Rappresenzione* November 29.

1979   Premiere of *Paradise Lost* at La Scala, Milan, conducted by the composer. Conducted *Paradise Lost* (Part II) before Pope John Paul II in Rome. *Overture, Vision and Finale* and *Adagietto*, both taken from *Paradise Lost*, performed in Salzburg. Received the Arthur Honegger Prize and honorary doctorate from Bourdeaux University.

30

1980   *Symphony #2* (Christmas Symphony), *Capriccio for Tuba, Te Deum, Lacrymosa.*

1981   *Agnus Dei* composed for the funeral of Stefán Cardinal Wyszynski.

1982   Conducted his works in Argentina, Australia, Brazil, New Zealand, Norway and Venezuela. *Concerto #2 for Violoncello and Orchestra.*

1983   Conducted the Washington National Symphony on his fiftieth birthday (November 23).

Notes

1. *Newsweek* magazine, March 17, 1969.
2. Harold Patton, "Penderecki, Composer for the Last Judgment," *Chicagoland and FM Guide* (April, 1968), 37.
3. Antes Orga, "Penderecki; Composer of Martyrdom," *Music and Musicians* XVIII (September, 1969), 34.
4. In a recent interview, the composer expressed the opinion that there were two rather than three style periods in his career as a composer. He tends to classify the early pieces—before 1960—as student pieces and states that his first style period begins with *Anaklasis* and *Threnody* (both completed in 1960) and goes up through *Magnificat* (1974). The second period starts with *The Awakening of Jacob* and continues to the present time. Interview with Krzysztof Penderecki; Village of Cross Keys, Baltimore, Maryland, March 31, 1982.
5. Antes Orga, "Krzysztof Penderecki," *Music and Musicians* XXII (October, 1973), 39.
6. Wolfram Schwinger, *Krzysztof Penderecki: List of Works* (Mainz: B. Schott's Söhne, 1980), 11.
7. European American Music Distributors Corp., 11 West End Road, Totowa, New Jersey 07512, is sole agent in the United States and Canada for B. Schott's Söhne and Moeck Verlag. All of the composer's works are published and released in the Eastern European countries under the PWM (Polskie Wydawnictwo Muzyczne) distributorship.

Bibliography *

BOOKS

Austin, William W. *Music in the 20th Century*. New York: W. W. Norton and Co., Inc., 1966.

Erhardt, Ludwik. *Contemporary Music in Poland*. Translated by Eugenia Tarska. Warsaw: Polonia Publishing House, 1966.

————. *Spotkania a Krzysztofem Pendereckim*. Krakow: Polskie Wydawnictwo Muzyczne, 1975.

Jarocinski, Stefán, editor. *Polish Music*. Warsaw: Polish Scientific Publishers, 1965.

Schwinger, Wolfram. *Penderecki: Begegnungen, Lebensdaten, Werkkomentare*. Stuttgart: Deutsche Verlagsantalt, 1979.

THESES (Unpublished)

Gebuhr, Ann Karen, "Stylistic Elements in Selected Works of Krzysztof Penderecki" (Unpublished Masters degree thesis, Indiana University, Bloomington, Indiana, 1970).

Hutcheson, Robert Joseph, Jr., "Twentieth Century Passion Settings: An Analytic Study of Max Baumann's *Passion*, Op. 63; Frank Martin's *Golgotha*; Krzysztof Penderecki's *St. Luke Passion*; and Ernest Pepping's *Passionbericht des Matthäus*" (Unpublished Ph.D. Thesis, Washington University, St. Louis, Missouri, 1976).

Linthicum, David Howell, "Penderecki's Notation: A Critical Evaluation" (Unpublished DMA thesis, University of Illinois, Urbana-Champaign, 1972).

Roberts, Gwen, "Sound Masses in Twentieth Century Music" (Un-

---

* *The items included in this brief bibliography are of a general nature. Articles on specific works are intentionally not included.*

published Ph.D. thesis, Indiana University, Bloomington, Indiana, 1978).

Tyra, Thomas H., "The Analysis of Three Twentieth Century Compositions for Wind Ensemble" (Unpublished DMA thesis, University of Michigan, Ann Arbor, 1971)

PERIODICAL AND NEWSPAPER ARTICLES

Cook, Eugene, "Penderecki: the Polish question—and others" (Interview), *Music Journal* XXXV (February, 1977), 8-10 ÷.

Dibelius, Ulrich, "Polische Avantgarde." *Melos* XXXIV (January, 1967), 7 ÷.

Erhardt, Ludwik, "A Glance at Contemporary Music in Poland," *Polish Music* XII, nos. 1-2 (1979), 22-24.

Grzenkowicz, Isabella, "Conversations with Krzysztof Penderecki," *Polish Music* XII, no. 3 (1977), 24-30; no. 4 (1977), 10-14.

Felder, David and Schneider, Mark, "An Interview with Krzysztof Penderecki," *The Composer* VIII (1976-77), 8-20.

Fleming, Shirley, "Musician of the Month, Krzysztof Penderecki," *Hi Fi/Musical America* XXV (December, 1975).

Hamilton, David, "Some Newer Figures in Europe," *Hi Fi/Musical America* XVIII (September, 1968), 55.

Honolka, Kurt, "Die Zukenft: normale Oper a la Rossini, Gesprach mit Krzysztof Penderecki," *Opern Welt* V (May, 1974), 36.

Jarocinski, Stefán, "Polish music after World War II," *Musical Quarterly* LI, no. 1 (January, 1965), 244-258.

Kolodin, Irving, "Penderecki's progress," *World* II (August 14, 1973), 42-43.

———, "The Passions of Penderecki," *Saturday Review* LI (February 24, 1968), 63-65.

Lewinski, Wolf-Eberhard von, "Where do we go from here? A European view," *Musical Quarterly* LV, no. 2 (1969), 198.

Marek, Tadeusz, "In Retrospect of the Last 30 Years; Contemporary Polish Composers," *Polish Music* VIII, no. 6 (1973), 6 ÷.

Newsweek Magazine, March 17, 1969.

Orga, Antes, "Krzysztof Penderecki," *Music and Musicians* XXII (October, 1973), 38-41.

————, "Penderecki: composer of martyrdom," *Music and Musicians* XVIII (September, 1969), 34-38.

Patton, Harold, "Penderecki, Composer for the Last Judgment," *Chicagoland and FM Guide* (April, 1969).

Schonberg, Harold C., "Penderecki's Aggressive Modernism," *New York Times* (March 7, 1969), 30.

Stocker, David A., "Some Observations and Perspectives on Music in Poland," *Choral Journal* XVIII (March, 1978), 31-35.

Zielinski, Tadeusz A., "Der einsame Weg des Krzysztof Penderecki," *Melos* XXIX (October, 1962), 318-323.